FRANCIS FRITH'S

CHATHAM
AND THE
MEDWAY TOWNS
PHOTOGRAPHIC MEMORIES

ALAN BIGNELL has spent more than forty years as a journalist in his native county of Kent, and was the winner of the Kent Journalist of the Year award in 1989. He is also the author of a dozen books about Kent and a similar number of others about different parts of the country. Alan now lives with his wife, Audrey, in the village of Barming, on the outskirts of Maidstone, where he continues to write about the county in which he has lived all his life.

FRANCIS FRITH'S
PHOTOGRAPHIC MEMORIES

CHATHAM AND THE MEDWAY TOWNS

PHOTOGRAPHIC MEMORIES

ALAN BIGNELL

First published in the United Kingdom in 2005 by
The Francis Frith Collection®

Limited hardback edition published in 2003
ISBN 1-85937-795-5

Paperback edition published in 2003
ISBN 1-85937-611-8

Reprinted in paperback 2006

Text and Design copyright The Francis Frith Collection®
Photographs copyright The Francis Frith Collection®
except where indicated.

The Frith® photographs and the Frith® logo are reproduced under licence from Heritage
Photographic Resources Ltd, the owners of the Frith® archive and trademarks.
'The Francis Frith Collection', 'Francis Frith' and 'Frith' are registered trademarks of
Heritage Photographic Resources Ltd.

All rights reserved. No photograph in this publication may be sold to a third party other
than in the original form of this publication, or framed for sale to a third party. No parts
of this publication may be reproduced, stored in a retrieval system, or transmitted, in any
form, or by any means, electronic, mechanical, photocopying, recording or otherwise,
without the prior permission of the publishers and copyright holder.

British Library Cataloguing in Publication Data

Chatham and the Medway Towns - Photographic Memories
Alan Bignell
ISBN 1-85937-611-8

The Francis Frith Collection
Frith's Barn, Teffont,
Salisbury, Wiltshire SP3 5QP
Tel: +44 (0) 1722 716 376
Email: info@francisfrith.co.uk
www.francisfrith.com

Printed and bound in Great Britain

Front Cover: **CHATHAM,** *Military Road c1960* C69049t
Frontispiece: **ROCHESTER,** *The Red Lion c1955* R44001

The colour-tinting is for illustrative purposes only, and is not intended to be historically accurate

Every attempt has been made to contact copyright holders of illustrative material. We will
be happy to give full acknowledgement in future editions for any items not credited. Any
information should be directed to The Francis Frith Collection.

AS WITH ANY HISTORICAL DATABASE THE FRITH ARCHIVE IS CONSTANTLY BEING
CORRECTED AND IMPROVED AND THE PUBLISHERS WOULD WELCOME INFORMATION
ON OMISSIONS OR INACCURACIES

CONTENTS

FRANCIS FRITH: VICTORIAN PIONEER	7
CHATHAM AND THE MEDWAY TOWNS - AN INTRODUCTION	10
CHATHAM TOWN CENTRE	14
THE RIVER MEDWAY	30
MILITARY AND NAVAL CONNECTIONS	36
BUCKMORE PARK	43
ROCHESTER	50
ACROSS THE RIVER	56
GILLINGHAM AND DISTRICT	70
INDEX	85
NAMES OF SUBSCRIBERS	88
Free Mounted Print Voucher	91

FRANCIS FRITH
VICTORIAN PIONEER

FRANCIS FRITH, founder of the world-famous photographic archive, was a complex and multi-talented man. A devout Quaker and a highly successful Victorian businessman, he was philosophical by nature and pioneering in outlook.

By 1855 he had already established a wholesale grocery business in Liverpool, and sold it for the astonishing sum of £200,000, which is the equivalent today of over £15,000,000. Now a very rich man, he was able to indulge his passion for travel. As a child he had pored over travel books written by early explorers, and his fancy and imagination had been stirred by family holidays to the sublime mountain regions of Wales and Scotland. 'What lands of spirit-stirring and enriching scenes and places!' he had written. He was to return to these scenes of grandeur in later years to 'recapture the thousands of vivid and tender memories', but with a different purpose. Now in his thirties, and captivated by the new science of photography, Frith set out on a series of pioneering journeys up the Nile and to the Near East that occupied him from 1856 until 1860.

INTRIGUE AND EXPLORATION

These far-flung journeys were packed with intrigue and adventure. In his life story, written when he was sixty-three, Frith tells of being held captive by bandits, and of fighting 'an awful midnight battle to the very point of surrender with a deadly pack of hungry, wild dogs'. Wearing flowing Arab costume, Frith arrived at Akaba by camel sixty years before Lawrence of Arabia, where he encountered 'desert princes and rival sheikhs, blazing with jewel-hilted swords'.

He was the first photographer to venture beyond the sixth cataract of the Nile. Africa was still the mysterious 'Dark Continent', and Stanley and Livingstone's historic meeting was a decade into the future. The conditions for picture taking confound belief. He laboured for hours in his wicker dark-room in the sweltering heat of the desert, while the volatile chemicals fizzed dangerously in their trays. Back in London he exhibited his photographs and was 'rapturously cheered' by members of the Royal Society. His reputation as a photographer was made overnight.

VENTURE OF A LIFE-TIME

Characteristically, Frith quickly spotted the opportunity to create a new business as a specialist publisher of photographs. He lived in an era of immense and sometimes violent change.

For the poor in the early part of Victoria's reign work was exhausting and the hours long, and people had precious little free time to enjoy themselves. Most had no transport other than a cart or gig at their disposal, and rarely travelled far beyond the boundaries of their own town or village. However, by the 1870s the railways had threaded their way across the country, and Bank Holidays and half-day Saturdays had been made obligatory by Act of Parliament. All of a sudden the working man and his family were able to enjoy days out and see a little more of the world.

With typical business acumen, Francis Frith foresaw that these new tourists would enjoy having souvenirs to commemorate their days out. In 1860 he married Mary Ann Rosling and set out on a new career: his aim was to photograph every city, town and village in Britain. For the next thirty years he travelled the country by train and by pony and trap, producing fine photographs of seaside resorts and beauty spots that were keenly bought by millions of Victorians. These prints were painstakingly pasted into family albums and pored over during the dark nights of winter, rekindling precious memories of summer excursions.

THE RISE OF FRITH & CO

Frith's studio was soon supplying retail shops all over the country. To meet the demand he gathered about him a small team of photographers, and published the work of independent artist-photographers of the calibre of Roger Fenton and Francis Bedford. In order to gain some understanding of the scale of Frith's business one only has to look at the catalogue issued by Frith & Co in 1886: it runs to some 670 pages, listing not only many thousands of views of the British Isles but also many photographs of most European countries, and China, Japan, the USA and Canada - note the sample page shown on page 9 from the hand-written Frith & Co ledgers recording the pictures. By 1890 Frith had created the greatest specialist photographic publishing company in the world, with over 2,000 sales outlets - more than the combined number that Boots and WH Smith have today! The picture on the next page shows the Frith & Co display board at Ingleton in the Yorkshire Dales (left of window). Beautifully constructed with a mahogany frame and gilt inserts, it could display up to a dozen local scenes.

POSTCARD BONANZA

The ever-popular holiday postcard we know today took many years to develop. In 1870 the Post Office issued the first plain cards, with a pre-printed stamp on one face. In 1894 they allowed other publishers' cards to be sent through the mail with an attached adhesive halfpenny stamp. Demand grew rapidly, and in 1895 a new size of postcard was permitted called the court card, but there was little room for illustration. In 1899, a year after Frith's death, a new card measuring 5.5 x 3.5 inches became the standard format, but it was not until 1902 that the divided back came into being, so that the address and message could be on one face and a full-size illustration on the other. Frith & Co were in the vanguard of postcard development: Frith's sons Eustace and Cyril continued their father's monumental task, expanding the number of views offered to the public and recording more and more places in Britain, as the coasts and countryside were opened up to mass travel.

Francis Frith had died in 1898 at his villa in Cannes, his great project still growing. The archive he created continued in business for another seventy years. By 1970 it contained over a third of a million pictures showing 7,000 British towns and villages.

FRANCIS FRITH'S LEGACY

Frith's legacy to us today is of immense significance and value, for the magnificent archive of evocative photographs he created provides a unique record of change in the cities, towns and villages throughout Britain over a century and more. Frith and his fellow studio photographers revisited locations many times down the years to update their views, compiling for us an enthralling and colourful pageant of British life and character.

We are fortunate that Frith was dedicated to recording the minutiae of everyday life, for it is this sheer wealth of visual data, the painstaking chronicle of changes in dress, transport, street layouts, buildings, housing, engineering and landscape that captivates us so much today. His remarkable images offer us a powerful link with the past and with the lives of our ancestors.

THE VALUE OF THE ARCHIVE TODAY

Computers have now made it possible for Frith's many thousands of images to be accessed almost instantly. Frith's images are increasingly used as visual resources, by social historians, by researchers into genealogy and ancestry, by architects and town planners, and by teachers involved in local history projects.

In addition, the archive offers every one of us an opportunity to examine the places where we and our families have lived and worked down the years. Highly successful in Frith's own era, the archive is now, a century and more on, entering a new phase of popularity. Historians consider the Francis Frith Collection to be of prime national importance. It is the only archive of its kind remaining in private ownership. Francis Frith's archive is now housed in an historic timber barn in the beautiful village of Teffont in Wiltshire. Its founder would not recognize the archive office as it is today. In place of the many thousands of dusty boxes containing glass plate negatives and an all-pervading odour of photographic chemicals, there are now ranks of computer screens. He would be amazed to watch his images travelling round the world at unimaginable speeds through internet lines.

The archive's future is both bright and exciting. Francis Frith, with his unshakeable belief in making photographs available to the greatest number of people, would undoubtedly approve of what is being done today with his lifetime's work. His photographs depicting our shared past are now bringing pleasure and enlightenment to millions around the world a century and more after his death.

CHATHAM AND THE MEDWAY TOWNS
AN INTRODUCTION

A relatively unobtrusive pavement sign shows where the single long, sinuous High Street leaves Rochester and enters Chatham, but today few people are aware of the distinction. The continuous North Kent riverside conurbation, with Chatham at its centre, Rochester and Strood to the west and Gillingham and Rainham to the east, was generally known as the Medway Towns, or even simply as Medway, long before officialdom acknowledged the fact and formally combined them under one local authority in 1998.

Yet even today, the characteristics that each of the towns developed remain recognisably distinct. Rochester, the oldest, is a typical cathedral city that wears the livery of its

GILLINGHAM, *Darland Banks c1960* G144037

history with a kind of jaunty dignity, while at the other end of the bridge that both joins and, curiously, separates them, there is an impatience about the way Strood bustles and jostles its way towards a destination it never seems to reach.

Despite the enthusiasm for modernity expressed in its Pentagon Shopping Centre, its pedestrian precincts, its impressive office blocks and its wide ring roads, Chatham has not yet entirely cast off the raffish air of the dockyard town that Charles Dickens knew, while there is a domesticity about Gillingham, of which Rainham is an extension, that reflects its predominantly residential character.

The only really common feature is the River Medway, from which the towns took their name and which gave them their identities from earliest times. Even before the late Stone Age settlement of the higher ground, out of reach of the floods that covered the lower marshes, people were fishing the river and hunting in the forested hills of its hinterland. The Romans captured the defended river crossing they called Durobrivae, now Rochester, and made it a port and supply base. When the Jutes arrived in Kent in the mid 5th century, they found a nearby village which they called Cetham, meaning a forest settlement.

After the arrival of Augustine and his monks in AD597, Rochester became Kent's second cathedral city; the nearby villages, including Chatham, shared in the prosperity that came from supplying the city with fish, agricultural and other products and services of all kinds. Over time, the river-borne trade with the increasingly voracious London markets became a more and more important element of the local economy. As the Medway came to be used more as a haven for sea-borne traffic, servicing the vessels that anchored in the river expanded the local economy further. Until the second half of the 16th century, however, the little town nevertheless remained virtually unknown to overland wayfarers, who passed it by on the Roman Watling Street from London to Dover.

Chatham Reach, that part of the River Medway where it gathers itself to escape into the Thames Estuary, shelters in a sharp bend behind a promontory that separates it from the more open, downstream, Gillingham Reach. Its position made it ideal as a place where Tudor warships could be laid up and where repairs could be carried out. There was a ready supply of timber which could be floated down the river from the Weald - the great primaeval forest that still covered much of Kent, Sussex and Surrey - to the very place where it was needed. Chatham was relatively easy to defend, especially after Upnor Castle, on the opposite bank, was built in 1567, although a hundred years later a Dutch fleet succeeded in breaching the defences and destroying and capturing naval ships in Chatham Reach.

After Chatham Dockyard was established as a base for Henry VIII's warships, the town expanded rapidly to house the great numbers of craftsmen and labourers that the new dockyard needed. It was this developing Chatham that the young Francis Drake would have known after his father, Edmund Drake, became prayer-reader to the fleet in the Medway in 1550. The family lived in one of the dismasted hulks that lay in the river then, until they moved to nearby Upchurch, where Edmund was vicar in 1560. During the war against Spain in the Netherlands, in the second half of the

16th century, Chatham's geography made it the country's premier royal dockyard. Probably the first ship built there was the little 56-ton *Sunne*, which sailed with the anti-invasion fleet assembled in the Medway estuary against the Spanish Armada in 1588.

From that time on, for most purposes Chatham was 'the dockyard', although even in 1774 the yard was quite small compared with its later size. Then, it was described as being 'on the south side of the River Medway, 15 miles from the entrance of it', where the river was 'so crooked that there is [sic] only six points of the compass for a wind with which ships of the line can sail down and ten to sail up, and that only for a few days during the spring tides.' Although the dockyard itself was said to be 'not of easy access', it had a longer waterfront than any of the other Royal yards and its 68-acre site gave plenty of room for buildings and other facilities.

Chatham grew rapidly throughout the 18th and 19th centuries. Of the many ships that were built there, the most famous of them all, the *Victory*, was launched in 1765. She was flagship for successive admirals both before and after Lord Nelson was killed aboard her at the Battle of Trafalgar in 1805.

After the defeat of Napoleon at Waterloo in 1815, Chatham continued to be a major shipbuilding yard. In 1817, Navy Pay Officer John Dickens was posted to the dockyard. He brought his family of three children, including his son Charles, to live first in a house in The Brook (since demolished to make way for the Pentagon Centre), then at No 2 Ordnance Terrace (later re-numbered 11) and finally at St Mary's Place. Charles Dickens then began his education at William Giles' school. It was the Chatham of this period that young Charles Dickens was describing when he wrote in *The Pickwick Papers* - the first instalment of which was published in 1836 - that the principal productions of the Medway Towns of Strood, Rochester, Chatham and Brompton (part of Gillingham) appeared to be soldiers, sailors, Jews, chalk, shrimps, officers and dockyardmen. The commodities chiefly exposed for sale in the public streets were marine stores, hardbake, apples, flatfish and oysters. Dickens wrote of the lively and animated appearance of the streets, and had Mr Pickwick observing that 'the smell which pervades the streets must be exceedingly delicious to those who are extremely fond of smoking.' Mr Pickwick went on to say of the four towns: 'A superficial traveller might object to the dirt, which is their leading characteristic; but to those who view it as an indication of traffic and commercial prosperity, it is truly gratifying.'

The Dickens family lived in Chatham for seven years before returning to London in 1822, but Charles came back to this part of Kent in 1856, when he bought Gad's Hill Place at nearby Higham, where he died in June 1870. Today, many of the shops in Rochester bear witness to the characters he created to people his fictional versions of the city.

In Dickens' day, the surrounding rural area was still mainly agricultural; what industry there was, beyond the dockyard, consisted of a few small paper mills, some independent boat building, a brickfield, some lime burning and a small chemicals factory. After 1850, though, Medway mud and chalk gouged out of the Downland hills made the area a major source of Portland cement, and there was also a huge increase in brickmaking and civil engineering.

The backbone of the local economy remained the dockyard, however, and throughout the 19th century, Chatham continued to be the largest British naval shipbuilding yard. In 1863, the *Achilles*, the first armoured battleship built in a British royal dockyard, and one of the largest warships in the world, was launched there, beginning a new era for the dockyard and the town. The arrival of iron-hulled vessels introduced new technology and new skills into ship-building, and a further 380 acres were added to the Chatham dockyard site. Nevertheless, when the first Dreadnought was launched at Portsmouth, Chatham once again had to re-invent itself, and after 1908 the dockyard specialised in building and servicing submarines.

Chatham's fortunes rose and fell with the tides of war and peace. After World War II - and a relatively short period of involvement with nuclear submarines - the dockyard was finally closed in 1984, ending nearly 300 years of royal dockyard history. The town staggered under the loss of 7,000 jobs, but immediately set about resurrecting itself as a late 20th-century industrial, commercial and tourist centre.

The old dockyard was split into three parts, each separately managed. One part, which lay in the neighbouring borough of Gillingham, became known as Chatham Maritime, and has been redeveloped as an industrial and residential area. Better-known is the older Georgian part, which under the supervision of the Chatham Historic Dockyard Trust, and now known as the World Naval Base, has become one of Kent's major tourist attractions. Fort Amherst, one of the dockyard's inland defences of the Napoleonic era, has been restored to become another attraction, and the town continues to hold annual Navy Days, just as it did before the dockyard closed.

In the 1960s, increasing traffic problems were eased by the opening of the Medway Towns by-pass - actually part of the M2 - and by the new town centre roads that came with the redevelopment of the area around The Brook. In May 1976, the town opened its landmark Pentagon Shopping Centre. The rapidly increasing population included many Londoners, who spilled out of the capital into major new peripheral residential developments, including the Warren Wood and Walderslade mini-towns south of Chatham.

The new Medway local authority created in 1974, which included the former Chatham borough, became the City of Rochester-upon-Medway in 1982, with Rochester retaining its separate city status within the new authority. It was not until 1998 that a long battle to gain administrative independence from the rest of Kent was rewarded with the creation of a new Medway Council, Kent's only autonomous unitary authority, independent of Kent County Council. It embraces a culturally diverse population of a quarter of a million people, and covers an area that stretches from Rainham to Strood and the Hoo Peninsula.

PHOTOGRAPHIC MEMORIES- CHATHAM AND THE MEDWAY TOWNS

CHATHAM TOWN CENTRE

CHATHAM, *High Street c1965* C69124

The glazed awning on the far left, was a feature of W H Smith's bookshops, and several of the shop fascias bear familiar names in distinctive styles. The window attracting the attention of the ladies on the right is that of Collier's, the furniture store, and the poster promising that 'Double Diamond Works Wonders' is on the side of The Bull public house.

CHATHAM, *High Street c1955* C69017

This part of the High Street is very different today, with The Sun Hotel gone from its Medway Street corner site. The dome further down the street was on the old Empire Theatre, which could seat 2,500 people. It specialised in music hall-style entertainment before it closed during the 1960s.

CHATHAM
The Town Hall and Military Road c1955
C69005

The virtual absence of motor traffic suggests that this photograph may have been taken in 1956, during the Suez Crisis petrol rationing, which did not end until the following year. The restrained architecture of The Eagle Tavern contrasts with that of both the Town Hall and the Chatham Constitution Club on the right of this picture.

CHATHAM TOWN CENTRE

◀ **CHATHAM**
*The Town Hall
c1960* C69050

The landmark clock tower has commanded attention from many parts of the town since it was built in 1899, but the building ceased to house council departments after 1974. The sailor approaching the bus stop on the left has probably walked down Dock Road from the dockyard, or has possibly just left the Royal Sailors' Club in Barrier Road, behind the Town Hall. Buses for Strood, Cobham and Meopham stop outside The Eagle Tavern, which has a still relatively rare television aerial.

▶ **CHATHAM**
*Military Road and the Town Hall
c1955* C69023

The town's naval links are illustrated by the Unifit outfitters, which advertises naval and civilian tailoring. The adjoining shop, displaying the Spratts Scottie dog, was that of Charles Carvell, bird dealer.

PHOTOGRAPHIC MEMORIES - CHATHAM AND THE MEDWAY TOWNS

CHATHAM TOWN CENTRE

CHATHAM
Military Road c1960
C69049

A No 147 bus waits outside The Eagle Tavern on the right, and on the left a fingerpost beyond the Imperial Forces public house points towards the public lavatories in Riverside Gardens.

PHOTOGRAPHIC MEMORIES - CHATHAM AND THE MEDWAY TOWNS

CHATHAM
Military Road c1960
C69062

National Service ended in 1960 and in this picture the first floor of Burton's men's outfitters shop on the corner of High Street and Military Road is still identified as the Combined Recruiting Centre, with the Medical Board premises on the second floor. The Red Lion opposite was soon to be demolished.

CHATHAM, *Military Road c1965* C69100
By now, The Red Lion (C69062) is replaced by the new block displaying the Betabake fascia beside the Salad Bowl fruit shop, with the Louis Francke ladies' hairdressing salon on the first floor, while opposite Montague Burton's has a closing-down sale. The No 142 bus, advertising Kent Life magazine, is bound for Weeds Wood via Huntsman's Corner.

CHATHAM TOWN CENTRE

CHATHAM, *Town Hall c1955* C69013
This view of the rear of the Town Hall is taken from Town Hall Gardens. From this point, the building shows the side fronting Wiffen's Avenue, with Rope Walk running along the bottom of the gardens.

▶ **CHATHAM**
*Town Hall
Gardens c1960*
C69075

The town's old graveyard behind the Town Hall had become very badly neglected by the beginning of the 20th century, so the gravestones were removed to line a boundary wall and the area was landscaped and opened as a public park.

◀ **CHATHAM**
*Town Hall
Gardens c1960*
C69083

The gardens are laid out on a site that slopes gently down towards Rope Walk and The Brook, offering a pleasant place in the centre of town in which to stroll or sit, and perhaps recover after a hard morning's shopping.

CHATHAM TOWN CENTRE

▲ **CHATHAM,** *Town Hall Gardens c1965* C69139

Five years after C69083 was taken, it would seem that a rubbish bin has been substituted for some of the seats, and at least one tree, on the left-hand side, has been felled. The man on the seat can stretch out his legs, knowing he will not be obstructing the path for cyclists, now banned.

◄ **CHATHAM**
The View from The Lines c1960 C69082

The significance of the River Medway in the life and development of Chatham is well illustrated in this view of the town and the river from the slopes of The Lines above Town Hall Gardens. Beyond and slightly to the right of the Town Hall we can just see the spire of Rochester Cathedral.

PHOTOGRAPHIC MEMORIES- CHATHAM AND THE MEDWAY TOWNS

▼ **CHATHAM,** *Victoria Gardens c1960* C69065

This was War Department land, beside New Road, and the venue for the fictional proposed duel between Mr Winkle and Dr Slammer in *The Pickwick Papers*, before the public gardens were opened in 1897 to celebrate the Diamond Jubilee of Queen Victoria.

► **CHATHAM**
St Bartholomew's Hospital c1960 C69072

St Bartholomew's was founded by Gundulf, Bishop of Rochester in 1078 for the city's lepers and sick poor. It is perhaps the oldest hospital in the country. Only part of it now remains, completely restored by Sir George Gilbert Scott, RA in 1874. Chatham's naval memorial spears the skyline in the centre of the picture.

CHATHAM TOWN CENTRE

◀ **CHATHAM**
New Road and the River Medway c1955
C69036

A mix of fairly elegant architectural styles line New Road opposite Fort Pitt Gardens, where a gardener tends the flowers beside the sign that marks Rochester's city boundary. The bus advertising the Trustee Savings Bank has just passed St Bartholomew's Hospital on the left, and Chatham's St Mary's church tower can be seen on the right.

▶ **CHATHAM**
New Road c1955
C69009

New in 1772, the road was built to bypass congested town centres from Star Hill, Rochester to the bottom of Chatham Hill. Fort Pitt Hill separates Rochester's Fort Pitt Gardens from Chatham's Victoria Gardens, where the town's 1920 war memorial stands in front of St Andrew's Presbyterian church, behind which are chalk quarries and the naval memorial.

CHATHAM
The Hospital of Sir John Hawkins, High Street c1960 C69056

The Chatham town sign stands outside the railings. The inscription over the door of the central building, behind the pump - now the lantern plinth - states that the hospital is in Chatham. Rebuilt as almshouses in 1840, they were converted into flats for up to 10 ex-Service pensioners and their families, and were formally opened by the late Queen Elizabeth the Queen Mother in 1984. They won a Civic Trust Award in 1986.

CHATHAM, *The View from the Great Lines c1955* C69030

Beginning with a series of ditches and bastions known as the Cumberland Lines in 1756, the Royal dockyard defences were extended later in the century. They became known as the Great Lines, including Fort Amherst, behind Chatham Town Hall, Fort Pitt and, in the 19th century, Fort Clarence. Designed to protect the docks from landward attack, they were never needed militarily, except for the kind of exercises Mr Pickwick (and his creator, Charles Dickens) witnessed, but they provide 90 acres of public open space between Chatham and Gillingham.

CHATHAM TOWN CENTRE

CHATHAM
The View from the Great Lines c1955
C69028

The slopes of the Lines offer a splendid vantage point from which to view the entire sweep of the Medway's Chatham Reach, from Chatham Town Hall in the foreground to Rochester Cathedral on the far side of the bend. The 'coolie's hat' roof identifies Sun Pier, with Kettle's Hard, Letley's Moorings and Suffrance Wharf beyond.

CHATHAM, *The View from the Great Lines c1955* C69029
From a slightly different viewpoint, this picture looks across Town Hall Gardens and the Chatham rooftops towards the Downs beyond. The scene is rather different today, when many of the buildings are no longer identifiable and others are hidden by new development.

PHOTOGRAPHIC MEMORIES - CHATHAM AND THE MEDWAY TOWNS

CHATHAM TOWN CENTRE

CHATHAM
The View from the Great Lines c1960 C69076

The Riverside Town Mills of W Hooker and Sons are situated just to the left of the stretch of water visible in this photograph. Flour milling was an important Chatham riverside industry, and there had been a mill and mill pond on this site since before 1066; but like so much else in the town, it is no more.

PHOTOGRAPHIC MEMORIES- CHATHAM AND THE MEDWAY TOWNS

THE RIVER MEDWAY

CHATHAM, *The River Medway c1965* C69129
The line of lighters moored in the river wait to be towed upstream. During the 1960s, 100 lighters a day went from Rochester to the upstream mills in trains of six, two deep.

PHOTOGRAPHIC MEMORIES- CHATHAM AND THE MEDWAY TOWNS

▼ **CHATHAM,** *The River Medway c1960* C69074

In this picture, the steeple of Rochester Cathedral seems to rise out of the castle keep in front of it, but it illustrates the strategic siting of the castle, overlooking the entire sweep of the approaches to the important crossing point at Rochester Bridge.

▶ **CHATHAM**
The Riverside c1965 C69146

Very much the same view as C69052 (Page 33), but a decade later, by which time the formerly grassed area had been paved and the glass shelter built. Wooden seats have replaced the old iron ones, but the fascination of the river for amateur photographers and for children is evidently unchanged.

THE RIVER MEDWAY

◀ **CHATHAM**
Gun Wharf Gardens c1955
C69052

Immediately below St Mary's church, practically the only surviving reminder that this was the site of the earliest Chatham Dockyard is Command House, the building with the five white-framed windows. Now an inn, it was built in 1758 as the residence of the officer in charge. Note the typically 1950s coach-sprung pram.

▶ **CHATHAM**
The River Medway c1965 C69141

The horizontal plume of smoke from the funnel of the ship moored off Sun Pier suggests that the glass shelter on the right might have offered welcome protection from an off-shore breeze, despite the sunshine being enjoyed by hardier river-watchers on the benches.

PHOTOGRAPHIC MEMORIES - CHATHAM AND THE MEDWAY TOWNS

CHATHAM
The View from the Pier c1965 C69123

The vessel moored to buoys against the far bank is probably unloading grain into a Town Mills silo. This view across the river separates Rochester Cathedral and the castle, giving a different outline from that in C69074 (page 32).

CHATHAM, *Riverside Gardens c1965* C69144
The gardens were laid out in the early 1960s on the former Gun Wharf, providing a welcome green space below the pinnacled tower of St Mary's parish church. The fashion in babies' prams has changed since that lady pushed hers along the riverside path.

THE RIVER MEDWAY

CHATHAM
*Riverside Gardens
c1965* C69142

Next to messing about on the river, few things are more relaxing than simply sitting on a bench and watching ships of all sizes go about their unhurried business. Just in case it is needed, a lifebuoy stands ready in its case on the extreme left of the picture.

CHATHAM, *The Riverside c1965* C69147

Ships of 300 to 4,000 tons lay at the fore and aft buoys in the river, while others tied up at wharves. These face different directions, perhaps waiting for the tide to turn before one heads downstream, towards the sea, and the others move on to discharge cargoes at one of the many riverside wharves. The swans are more interested in whether or not anyone in Riverside Gardens will share a sandwich with them.

PHOTOGRAPHIC MEMORIES- CHATHAM AND THE MEDWAY TOWNS

MILITARY AND NAVAL CONNECTIONS

CHATHAM, *HM Dockyard, The Main Gate c1955* C69014

The almost intimidating main gate in Dock Road was built in 1719; the Royal arms in coloured relief above the main arch are those of George III, added in 1811. Cannon-barrel bollards protect the brickwork, and a speed restriction sign limits vehicular speed to 20mph. The figurehead, which may represent the Duke of Wellington or his brother, Richard Wellesley, was salvaged after HMS *Wellesley* (1815) was sunk by enemy action during the Battle of Britain in September 1940.

MILITARY AND NAVAL CONNECTIONS

CHATHAM
The Royal Marines Barracks, the Officers' Quarters c1955 C69015

The Royal Marines were linked with Chatham from 1755 until the 1950s, when their Gun Wharf barracks were demolished and the site redeveloped for Lloyds of London offices. The officers' quarters were in Dock Road, where this Royal Marine stands guard.

CHATHAM, *Dock Road and St Mary's Church* c1955 C69016

The old Chatham parish church overlooks the Gun Wharf from a site originally occupied by a Saxon church. Despite major restoration of the 18th century building in 1903, it became redundant in 1974. The two soldiers passing the Fort Amherst site are probably Royal Engineers on their way back to the School of Military Engineering.

CHATHAM, *The Royal Naval Memorial c1955* C69019

There is an impressive dignity about the globe-crowned, lion-guarded obelisk that was unveiled by HRH the Duke of Windsor in July 1922. From its high point on the Great Lines, it is a readily distinguished landmark from afar.

MILITARY AND NAVAL CONNECTIONS

CHATHAM
The Royal Naval Memorial c1960 C69081

This view shows the whole monument, including the memorial walls and domed pavilion wings, inside the tended enclosure. The inscription reads: 'In honour of the Navy and to the abiding memory of these ranks and ratings of this port who laid down their lives in the defence of this empire and have no other grave than the sea.'

BROMPTON, *The Crimean Memorial Arch 1894* 34042

Below the memorial inscription over the main arch, the Royal Engineers' motto 'Ubique' ('Everywhere'), flanks the Latin inscription 'Quo Fas Et Gloria Ducant' ('Whither Right and Glory Lead'). The triple arch memorial to men of the Corps was erected in Brompton Barracks in 1860. On the right, a soldier stands guard at the entrance to the barrack square.

BROMPTON, *The Royal Engineers' Barracks 1894* 34041

Brompton Barracks were built in 1804-06, originally for artillerymen, and became the headquarters of the Royal Engineers when the School of Military Engineering was founded there in 1812. Although wholly in Gillingham, it was known as the Chatham School until 1962, when Queen Elizabeth II granted it the 'Royal' title. In this picture, the men on parade wear the uniform of the period, complete with spiked helmet, and the horse-drawn vehicle standing beside the post box, outside the pillared portico, may await an officer leaving the building.

MILITARY AND NAVAL CONNECTIONS

BROMPTON, *The Gordon Memorial and the R E Institute 1894* 34043

One of the most distinctive features of Brompton Barracks is this very unusual variation of more common equestrian statues, with General Gordon, mounted on a richly caparisoned camel. The General died in 1885 and this statue, erected in 1890, faces the Memorial Arch (see 34042, page 41).

PHOTOGRAPHIC MEMORIES- CHATHAM AND THE MEDWAY TOWNS

BUCKMORE PARK

CHATHAM, *Buckmore Park c1960* C69088

Opened in May 1953 by its founder, then Scoutmaster (now Park Superintendent) Cecil Whitehead, the Scout Centre on the southern edge of Chatham embraced 60 acres of woodland, leased to the Scout Movement by the Rochester Bridge Trust. The ex-army Nissen hut behind the vehicle was the first building on the site, and was used for volunteer staff accommodation and the shop until the Admin Building in the foreground, which included the Camp Hospital, was built.

► CHATHAM
Buckmore Park c1960 C69093

Originally, all the buildings except the Admin Block were sited among the woodland that comprised most of the 60-acre site. Today, nearer 200 acres are administered by the Buckmore Park Medway and Strood Scout Centre, a charity, and Buckmore Park Services, a limited company.

◄ CHATHAM
Buckmore Park, the Providore c1960
C69090

The fingerpost directs visitors to various on-site amenities, including the Warden's Office, the Providore (the shop) with its familiar Walls ice cream sign, and the First Aid and Hospital hut, easily identified by the prominently displayed Red Cross.

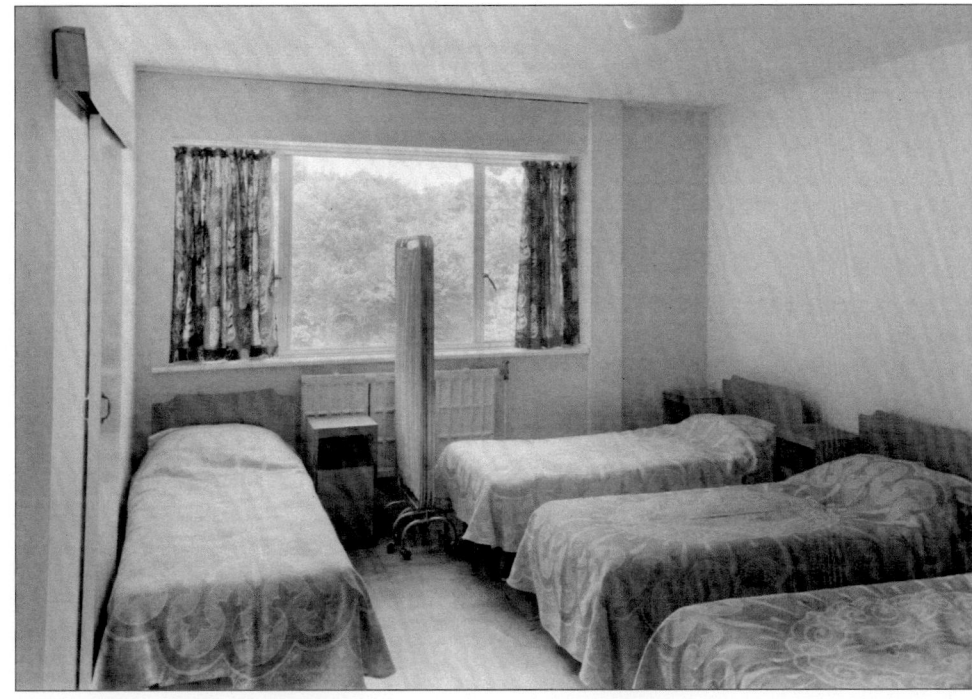

▲ **CHATHAM,** *Buckmore Park, the Hospital c1960* C69086

Hospital staff dealt with all the relatively minor mishaps to be expected from camp life, from treating wasp stings and bruises to suturing small cuts. Bed space was not generous, but who needed it, when there were so many outdoor activities to encourage patients' quick recovery?

◀ **CHATHAM**
*Buckmore Park,
the Swimming Pool
c1960* C69084

The large indoor heated swimming pool, opened in 1957, was one of the first and the largest privately-owned pools of its kind in the country, complete with springboard and three-stage diving boards. The side windows were subsequently filled in as a heat conservation measure. The notice bans balls and flippers from the pool.

PHOTOGRAPHIC MEMORIES - CHATHAM AND THE MEDWAY TOWNS

▼ **CHATHAM,** *Buckmore Park, the HQ c1965* C69099

This picture shows the back of the Admin Building (C69088, pages 44-45) which housed the administration office, the shop and the hospital, and also provided some staff accommodation. The telephone kiosk was a convenience; the television aerial by now a must.

► **CHATHAM**
Buckmore Park, Camp Activities c1965 C69113

In the 1960s, camping was the most important of all scouting activities, and Scout and Cub groups - no Guides until the late 1960s - brought their own tents and other equipment to the open camp site amid the woodland. Here, some of the boys write their journals or letters home, while others go about the housekeeping chores.

BUCKMORE PARK

◀ **CHATHAM**
Buckmore Park, Pioneering an Aerial Ropeway c1965 C69115

Scouts did not wear their uniforms while they enjoyed the many different activities available to them at the park, but they did have to give personal belongings an airing outside their tents. The CND (Campaign for Nuclear Disarmament) sign at the side of the camp site shows the movement had its supporters among Scouts, too.

▶ **CHATHAM**
Buckmore Park, the Cub Huts c1965
C69117

These Cub accommodation huts were ex-service huts made of corrugated asbestos, brought to the park as 'flat packs' to be bolted together on site. At this time, the youngest Cubs would have been about eight years old, but these seem to have been joined by younger children, probably the children of staff.

PHOTOGRAPHIC MEMORIES- CHATHAM AND THE MEDWAY TOWNS

CHATHAM
*Buckmore Park,
Tracking c1965* C69109

Kent is a maritime county, and that, together with the centuries-old local naval tradition, meant that Sea Scouts were as much in evidence at Buckmore Park as any others. All boys enjoy woodland tracking, even if it is not a skill much needed at sea.

CHATHAM, *Buckmore Park, Scouting Activities c1965* C69111
Basic housekeeping is a requirement of any well-organised camp, and these boys carry out their chores under watchful adult eyes. The Centre's shorts-only rule applied to everyone, partly as a security measure to distinguish authorised from any unauthorised users.

CHATHAM, *Buckmore Park, the Camp Fire c1965* C69104
No Scout or Cub camp could be complete without the traditional camp fire to end the day. The Native American headdresses suggest that this particular day's end followed the equally traditional Wide Game. Notwithstanding the 'shorts only' rule, some of the boys found comfort from a blanket draping their knees.

PHOTOGRAPHIC MEMORIES- CHATHAM AND THE MEDWAY TOWNS

ROCHESTER

ROCHESTER, *High Street 1908* 59875

Not a hatless head to be seen as the open-top tram, en route to Frindsbury across the river, passes the lantern and railings of Eastgate House, threatening conflict with horse-drawn traffic. Gas lights overhang the crammed shop windows of the timbered building that became Mr Sapsea's house in Charles Dickens' last, unfinished, book *The Mystery of Edwin Drood*. At No 146, there are more gas lights to illuminate Fred Willows' pawnbroker's shop, with the traditional three golden balls over the door. The Chatham, Rochester and Gillingham Observer had been the local newspaper since 1870.

ROCHESTER
The Cathedral 1894 34012

The Norman west front of England's second oldest cathedral, after Canterbury, is one of the best of its kind, with a finely sculpted main doorway and a 15th-century window the Victorians restored as a memorial to Royal Engineers who died in the Afghan and South African wars. In this picture, the building has quite recently been rescued from near ruin with a restoration that included the removal of the spire in 1823 and the addition of the tower pinnacles. Ships of all sizes crowd the river in the background.

ROCHESTER, *The Castle 1894* 34034
The castle grounds were laid out as public gardens in 1870, and the ladies on the benches may well be nannies, enjoying the sunshine with their young charges. Older children could buy bags of corn for a few pennies from the caretaker's house with which to feed the birds.

ROCHESTER, *College Gate and the Cathedral 1908* 59881

The photographer aroused plenty of curiosity as he pictured the structure also variously known as Cemetery Gate, Chertsey's Gate and Jasper's Gate. This last name was a legacy of Charles Dickens, who made the 18th-century weatherboarded house over the gate the home of church organist John Jasper in *The Mystery of Edwin Drood*. This picture, taken from the High Street, also shows the adjoining building; in Dickens' last novel, it became the home of chief verger Mr Tope. The cathedral, its spire restored in 1904, can be seen behind it.

PHOTOGRAPHIC MEMORIES - CHATHAM AND THE MEDWAY TOWNS

▼ **ROCHESTER,** *College Gate c1955* R44093

This is the College Yard side of the gate, looking through to the High Street and Northgate (formerly Pump Lane). The 15th-century gateway was one of several that once gave access to the 11th-century Priory of St Andrew. In this picture, there is a television aerial attached to the chimney, and the sign on the pillar box points the way to the Post Office. The bow-fronted house squeezed between the gate and the terrace of houses on the right offers luncheons and teas.

▶ **ROCHESTER**
The Red Lion c1955
R44001

The bus advertises Fremlins' ales outside the Red Lion, a Style & Winch house of flamboyant grandeur, but now no more, sad to say. There are now traffic lights and a great deal more traffic where this policeman stands on point duty at the junction of High Street with Corporation Street (left) and Star Hill (right).

ROCHESTER

◀ **ROCHESTER**
High Street c1955
R44034

The trams have given way to buses and the horse-drawn vehicles to motorcars, and hatless heads are now commonplace. Blundells at No 135 advertises post-war Utility furniture, and Belisha beacons have joined the street furniture to identify pedestrian crossings. The buildings otherwise remain very much as they were half a century earlier (see 59875, pages 52-53) and, in many cases, long before that.

▶ **ROCHESTER**
The Bridge c1955 R44040

The River Medway traditionally separates the Men of Kent on its east side from the Kentish Men on the west, but bridges such as this one unite the two 'tribes'. There has been a bridge at Rochester since Roman times, connecting Rochester and Chatham with cross-Medway Strood, but in 1914 a new bridge was built on top of the 19th-century one, which was then removed. That bridge was joined in the 1960s by the dual carriageway box-girder road bridge and footway alongside.

ACROSS THE RIVER

ROCHESTER
*The Castle and the Cathedral from Strood
1894* 34030

Steam and sail together characterise the changes taking place at the end of the 19th century. There are far fewer of the traditional Medway bawleys (fishing boats) now than there once were, and across the river, the pinnacled cathedral tower is still without its steeple, which was not restored until 1904.

PHOTOGRAPHIC MEMORIES - CHATHAM AND THE MEDWAY TOWNS

STROOD
General View c1955
S541011

Only the large building just left of the bridge approach remains of the Aveling and Porter steam traction engines factory, taken over in 1934 by Wingets engineering works, seen here. The site is now occupied by Medway's Civic Centre.

STROOD, *High Street c1955* S541001

Early chain stores, including Home and Colonial Stores, International Tea Stores and Boots the Chemist, were all represented in Strood High Street by now; but older shops, like Mence Smith (on the left), still catered for the home handyman before the DIY superstores arrived, while the radio shop also sold bicycles - perhaps to some of the cyclists emerging from Commercial Road.

ACROSS THE RIVER

STROOD
The River Medway
c1955 S541012

The river is littered with leisure craft and mooring buoys, and the sheds of the Holbourn-Eaton engineering works corrugate the roofscape on the far (Strood) side. The white roofs on the far left are those of Morgan's woodyard.

FRINDSBURY, *All Saints' Church c1960* F157002
Much vandalised in the 1950s, the prominent but isolated old church became one of the first in the Rochester diocese to lock its doors when not in use and the first to install an alarm system. The workman on the scaffolding against the tower, however, is more probably repairing the ravages of time, the most relentless vandal of all.

PHOTOGRAPHIC MEMORIES- CHATHAM AND THE MEDWAY TOWNS

▼ **HOO,** *The Village c1955* H356015

Although since 1968 this place has been Hoo St Werburgh, to distinguish it from other Hoo Peninsula villages, it is still generally known simply as Hoo. In this picture, the camera is looking down Church Street from High Street (renamed Stoke Road in 1959). The Five Bells public house is on the corner of Bells Lane, on the left, and further along, the building with the balcony is the former Victory Inn.

► **HOO**
The Church c1955
H356009

The spire, seen here from the back of the church, has been a landmark for mariners for centuries. The churchyard is where Thomas Aveling (see S541011, page 60) was buried in 1882. The church clock was presented by Mr Warwick Stunt in thanks for his wife's recovery from a serious illness in 1892.

ACROSS THE RIVER

◀ **HOO**
The Church and the Chequers Hotel c1950
H356006

There have been changes in Church Street since the 1950s, but The Chequers, like the church, is still there. The solitary car stands outside the former school, set back behind the houses, which is now the local library.

▶ **HOO**
The River c1955
H356041

Sailing barges and leisure craft rub hulls in this typical riverside scene, and the more recent development of the marina amply demonstrates that there is still nothing - absolutely nothing - half so much worth doing as simply messing about in boats.

PHOTOGRAPHIC MEMORIES - CHATHAM AND THE MEDWAY TOWNS

▶ **CLIFFE**
High Street c1950
C464014

The old town of Cliffe, destroyed by fire in 1520, was revived briefly by the cement industry in the second half of the 19th century. This part of the village has remained something of a period piece ever since then. The Parker's shop window displays advertisements for products as diverse as Brasso and Bluebell metal polishes, Mansion Polish for tiled floors and Silver Shred marmalade, while further down, the Victoria and Black Bull public houses testify to Victorian thirsts.

◀ **CLIFFE**
Oast Houses c1955
C464012

Scenes like this, so typical of rural Kent, became rare after the mid-century decline of hop growing made hundreds of oast houses ripe for conversion. New varieties of fruit trees changed the character of traditional orchards, and a few free-ranging chickens came to be regarded as an uneconomic anachronism.

▲ **SHORNE,** *The Post Office c1955* S530010

The typically Kentish peg-tiled roof, with its garnish of houseleek and lichen, would have been known to Charles Dickens, for whom a favourite walk was from his Gad's Hill home near Strood to Shorne. The building is now a private house, its responsibilities usurped by more modern shops a little further along the road to the left.

◄ **COBHAM**
The Hall 1899 44238

A late Elizabethan and 18th-century mansion described as one of the most important houses in Kent. Now a girls' boarding school, the house was once the seat of the Earls of Darnley, and includes interior features by James Wyatt, Inigo Jones, and the Adam brothers.

PHOTOGRAPHIC MEMORIES- CHATHAM AND THE MEDWAY TOWNS

COBHAM
High Street c1960
C130051

On the left, the post office advertises orange squash, and G W Gander's grocery and provisions shop opposite probably provided pretty well everything else. The Darnley Arms, the oldest public house in Cobham, claims to date from 1196; it is reputedly haunted by Sir Thomas Kemp, who spent his last days there after being reprieved from execution in Rochester.

COBHAM, *The Leather Bottle 1894* 34046
Sixty years after featuring in Dickens' *The Pickwick Papers*, the inn had become The Old Pickwick Leather Bottle. The pub sign depicted Mr Pickwick himself, and patrons could take meals in the Charles Dickens Pickwick Room. The adjoining general store of R Usher was made prominent by its distinctive chequered brickwork.

ACROSS THE RIVER

COBHAM
The Leather Bottle
c1955 C130037

Sixty years after 34046 (page 66), the cladding has been stripped from the walls of the inn to reveal old timbers, and the approval of motoring organisations is prominently displayed. The narrowness of the street and the almost complete absence of pedestrian pavements makes the 'Waiting Prohibited' signs by the bus stop very necessary.

COBHAM, *The Church 1899* 44241
The windmill is long gone, but the 12th-century church, to which the tower was added later, is famous for its pavement of 20 brasses dating from 1320 to 1529. The chimneys belong to the 16th-century New College almshouses alongside the church.

PHOTOGRAPHIC MEMORIES- CHATHAM AND THE MEDWAY TOWNS

▼ **COBHAM,** *The Hall 1899* 44239

By far the most impressive building in the parish, the Tudor mansion, with its octagonal wing turrets and a 50 acre park landscaped by Humphrey Repton in 1790, was the result of the redevelopment of a smaller house by the 10th Lord Cobham. Queen Elizabeth I slept here in 1559, and so did Charles II and his new bride in 1660. In 1882, it was to Cobham Hall that English cricketers brought the Ashes from Australia for the first time. The Hall became a girls' school in 1957.

▶ **HALLING**
The School c1955
H350005

Children cross open fields to the school that was opened in 1876, and where gas lighting was replaced with electricity in 1952. The chalk scars in the landscape beyond are a reminder that this is one of the Medway-side villages that owes much to the 19th-century cement industry.

ACROSS THE RIVER

◄ **SNODLAND**
*Holborough Road
c1960* S535026

The camera looks towards The Bull (right) on the corner of the High Street where it separates Malling Road from Holborough Road, and The Bricklayers' Arms is on the left just past the shops. The tobacconist and newsagent has a pavement weighing machine outside its door.

► **SNODLAND**
The Station c1960
S535030

The railway arrived in Snodland in 1856, connecting Maidstone West with Strood. Thereafter Snodland quickly grew from a quiet, almost wholly agricultural village, into a small town, fed by the two main industries: cement and paper-making. By 1960 the population was well over 12,000, and it is much more today.

PHOTOGRAPHIC MEMORIES - CHATHAM AND THE MEDWAY TOWNS

SNODLAND
Mulberry Cottage c1965
S535032

Named for the mulberry tree that grew in the garden, this 18th-century Kentish hall house in the High Street was once at the centre of Snodland, where the market cross stood outside The Red Lion inn opposite. In the 1920s, the cottage was stripped to its skeleton and rebuilt, using original materials wherever possible.

PHOTOGRAPHIC MEMORIES - CHATHAM AND THE MEDWAY TOWNS

GILLINGHAM AND DISTRICT

GILLINGHAM, *High Street c1960* G144021

Gillingham's High Street is wider than those of either Chatham or Rochester, and the town was virtually created by the need to house workers after the major Victorian extension of the Royal Dockyard. At the time this picture was taken, the dockyard was still by far the largest single employer. This view looks past the King Street junction and the Mr Samuel Pepys public house towards the railway station, which boasts of frequent electric services to Chatham and other destinations.

PHOTOGRAPHIC MEMORIES- CHATHAM AND THE MEDWAY TOWNS

GILLINGHAM AND DISTRICT

GILLINGHAM
High Street c1960
G144033

The station is behind the camera in this alternative view of the High Street. The bus stop outside the Britannia public house is for bus numbers 26, 26A, 39 and 40; opposite, a No 26 bus heads for Gravesend. The architecture reflects the Victorian character of the town, but the bunting gives no clue to its reason for being there.

PHOTOGRAPHIC MEMORIES- CHATHAM AND THE MEDWAY TOWNS

▶ **GILLINGHAM**
The Strand c1955
G144010

A sign in the river warns of hidden dangers for swimmers and small boats, but ashore there were plenty of safe ways to enjoy a summer's day on this pleasant, green, riverside corridor at the northern end of the town. The Strand was named in 1924, extended in 1930, and throughout the 1950s and 1960s, summer found the foreshore as crowded as any seaside beach.

◀ **GILLINGHAM**
The Miniature Railway c1955
G144016

As well as the ever-popular ball games, picnics and simply watching the boats go by, the Strand at Gillingham also offered a paddling pool, a boating pool, a children's playground, miniature golf, a municipal swimming pool from the late 1930s, and after 1948, this Lilliputian miniature railway.

GILLINGHAM AND DISTRICT

▲ **GILLINGHAM,** *By the Medway c1955* G144043

For away-from-it-all families, the open parkland extension of the Strand was ideal for a quiet riverside picnic, where the children could don bathing trunks and enjoy the unique delight of Medway mud squelching between their toes.

◄ **GILLINGHAM**
Darland Banks c1960
G144037

In 1933, 70 acres of chalk downland were acquired by Chatham and Gillingham councils to create this beautiful open countryside nature reserve between the two towns. The local wildlife includes several species of orchids and butterflies. At the centre of this picture, we can see the horses of travellers whose mobile homes are among the trees.

PHOTOGRAPHIC MEMORIES- CHATHAM AND THE MEDWAY TOWNS

GILLINGHAM AND DISTRICT

GILLINGHAM
By the Medway c1955
G144344

This is the river near the Strand in Gillingham, and is very much as the young Francis Drake might have known it. The river was very popular with both swimming clubs, and individual swimmers in the first half of the 20th century.

PHOTOGRAPHIC MEMORIES - CHATHAM AND THE MEDWAY TOWNS

GILLINGHAM
Twydall Green c1960
G144031

The Twydall residential area was developed mainly by Gillingham borough council between 1948 and 1965, and the Green became the area's shopping centre. These newly-built shops include the Co-op, displaying children's clothes, and the International Stores, which protects its window display of groceries with a striped awning. Motor scooters were a popular alternative to cars and bicycles at the time this picture was taken.

UPCHURCH, *The Village c1955* U46015

Although actually very old, this is another Medway-side village that was left with a distinctly Victorian appearance by the 19th century building boom, when it was a source of brick earth and also chalk for cement making. The infants' school, built in 1881, forms a village centre with the church and The Crown Inn.

UPCHURCH, *The Church of St Mary the Virgin c1955* U46008

The most distinctive feature of the church is its curious 'candle-snuffer' two-tier steeple, but the village also remembers that in 1560, its vicar was Edmund Drake, father of Francis Drake. Seventeen years later, Francis Drake began the historic round-the-world voyage that earned him his knighthood in 1581.

PHOTOGRAPHIC MEMORIES - CHATHAM AND THE MEDWAY TOWNS

GILLINGHAM AND DISTRICT

UPCHURCH
Otterham Quay c1955
U46011

The sailing barges look very much at home bottomed-out on the creek mud. From the 1830s to the 1930s, barges like this brought manure from London for the fields, and gasworks ash and other refuse for the local brickworks. The barges would return to the metropolis with up to 80 tons of mud for the cement works, or with locally-made bricks demanded by the hugely expanding capital.

RAINHAM
High Street c1955
R80001

The shops bristle with advertisements for Gold Flake, Woodbine and Capstan cigarettes; for cafés and for Ucal chemist products. Opposite them, before Ivy Street, evening newspaper readers are spoiled for choice: the pavement board promotes Friday's Evening News serial by Ruby M Ayres, 'People In Love', and at the same time urges customers to 'Get your Star here'.

RAINHAM, *Station Road c1955* R80004

In this view from the High Street, a man sits under the awning outside the Rainham and District Co-operative Society shop, opposite the wine merchant's shop of J Owen Carter. Frank Rule's newsagent (extreme left) displays a pavement board announcing a new Dan Dare serial in the boys' comic, the *Eagle*.

RAINHAM, *St Margaret's Parish Church c1955* R80012

The first stone church on this site, just beside the old Watling Street, was built soon after 1066, but the present building is mainly 13th-century, with a rather handsome 15th-century stepped-buttressed beacon tower. The original roof beams and doors remain, but the stained glass is Victorian.

PHOTOGRAPHIC MEMORIES - CHATHAM AND THE MEDWAY TOWNS

RAINHAM
London Road c1950 R80010

Trees line one side, and telegraph poles the other side of this section of the A2 from Rainham to Gillingham, where Mrs Hall had her hairdresser's shop, E H Chatfield was the confectioner and Len Button the butcher. Zebra crossings gave pedestrians priority over vehicles from 1951, but the little dog on the right has other priorities; the number of pedestrians would seem to present no problems to either the disappearing horse-drawn vehicle or the approaching cyclist.

BREDHURST, *The Village c1955* B582003

The shop with the telephone kiosk outside, the van, and the electricity supply lines dispel some of the timelessness that clings to one of the area's more remote villages, where The Bell inn has refreshed its customers (although not always with Style & Winch beers) since Tudor times.

INDEX

CHATHAM

Dock Road 37
General View 23, 26, 27, 28-29
Great Lines 26, 27, 28-29
Gun Wharf Gardens 33
H M Dockyard 36
High Street 14-15, 16
Hospital of Sir John Hawkins 26
Military Road 16, 17, 18-19, 20
New Road 24-25
R E Institute 41
River Medway 30-31, 32, 33, 34, 35
Riverside Gardens 34, 35
Royal Marines Barracks 37
Royal Naval Memorial 38, 39
St Bartholomew's Hospital 24
St Mary's Church 37
Town Hall 16, 17, 21
Town Hall Gardens 22-23
Victoria Gardens 24

BROMPTON

Crimean Memorial Arch 39
Gordon Memorial 41
Royal Engineers' Barracks 40

AROUND CHATHAM

Bredhurst 84
Buckmore Park 42-43, 44-45, 46-47, 48, 49
Cliffe 62-63
Cobham 63, 64, 65, 66
Frindsbury 59
Gillingham 10, 70-71, 72-73, 74-75, 76-77, 78
Halling 66
Hoo 60-61
Rainham 82, 83, 84
River Medway 75, 76-77, 78-79
Rochester 50-51, 52, 53, 54-55, 56-57
Shorne 63
Snodland 66-67, 68-69
Strood 58, 59
Upchurch 78, 79, 80-81

NAMES OF SUBSCRIBERS

Derrick R. Acott, Rochester
Neil & Nicola Alexander, Chatham
Albert Allard, Chatham
John H. C. Allen, Rainham
Jack Arnold, Chatham
Susan Anne Ashdown, Chatham
Leslie N. Ashdown, Chatham
Stephen R. Austen, Chatham
Gwen (Hunt) Baker, Ipswich
John Baker
Valerie H. Barden, Rochester
Mrs Joyce Boughton, Gillingham
G. & J. Bradford, Rainham
Mrs R. Bradley, Chatham
Mrs Doris Broom
William John Brunt, Chatham
Theresa A. Bryan, Chatham
Paul David Budden
Derek M. Burchett, Strood
Geoffrey G. Burchett, Canterbury
Nigel J.A. Burke, Rainham
Kieren V. Burling
Dr. Burns, Rochester
Stan Campbell, Chatham
Colin W. S. Caney, Rochester
Leiann T. Clarke, Chatham
Sheila E. Clarke, Rochester
Stephen P. Clarke, Chatham
Joan May Cook nee Tanner
D. Dance, Rochester
Eric L. Dene
Mrs J. A. Dexter, Chatham

Martha & John Dollin
A. N. Eames, Gillingham
Emma Everitt, Chatham
Dr & Mrs Stuart Fair, Lordswood, Chatham
Stephen W. Fielding, Walderslade, Chatham
C. K. Ford
Douglas C. Francis, Gillingham
Peter A. Garlinge, Chatham
Dave & Val Garrett
Phil Garrett
Mr & Mrs James Gay
Kenneth Ernest Gibbs, Rochester
Miss Susan Gilby, Lordswood
Alan R. Glanville
Michael Glanville, Gillingham
Shane Goldup, Rochester
J. M. Gollop
Harry & Ellen Goodier (Deceased)
Rita K. Hadlow
Derek J. Hallewell, formerly Chatham
Laurence & Catherine Hannaford
Simon & Lucy Hannaford
Marguerite Hannaford
Richard & Angela
Brian Harrington, Chatham, Kent
Derek Harris, Rochester
P. E. Harris, Rochester
Andrew Hart, Rochester
John F. Hart, Strood
Mrs Alice Hayes, Cuxton
Jill Heard
A. T. Hedges

Rita and Dave Howes
Janet E. Hukins, Rochester
Mrs P. A. Hulatt, Rochester
Francis L. Ince
Miss L. James, Gillingham
Paul Anthony Jarrett, Chatham
Colin A. Jarvis
Dave Jones & Family, Chatham
Carol Juniper, Rochester, Kent
Helen Kennett, Chatham
Stanley L. Kennett
Derek G. King
Brenda Landers, Chatham
Mr David Lane, Chatham
Edward Lane, son of Mary & Herbert
John J. Laraman, Rochester
Simon P. Laraman, Rochester
Frank Robert Lewis
Raymond M. Liston
Keith A. Mantle
Dorothy Martin
Andrew M. Massey
D. E. Maynard, Chatham
Chris J. Meeds, Chatham
Dr. & P. R. Melhuish
Karen J. Melhuish, Walderslade, Chatham
Mike Mitchell, Wigmore
David & Annette Morgan, Rainham
Mr F. W. Nicholson, Rainham
Alan G. Norcutt, Rochester
Graham Owen, Chatham
Mrs Pamela Penfold & Mr David Penfold
Graeme M. Pike, Walderslade
T. A. Pocock
Mr & Mrs A. Purcell, Wainscott

Linda Rayfield, Chatham
Mrs G. M. Read, Chatham
Terence Bryn Reece, Chatham
Philip Rhodes
Richard & Linda Roberts, Chatham
William Roper, Rainham
David James Ruck
Jennifer Russell
John Salmon, Walderslade
Alfred C. Salt
G. Saunder, Gillingham
Dennis J. Scott, Chatham
Mr & Mrs G. F. Simpson, Chatham
Brian James Skinner, Lordswood
Norman B. Spary, Lordswood
Alfred E. Stevens, Chatham
John W. Thompson, Rochester
Mina Walledge-Payne, Rochester
Donald William Walsh, Rochester, Kent
John H. Ward, Chatham
John Warren, Lordswood
Brian D. Weeden, P/Const. Rtd
John W. Weeks, Chatham
David Welsh, Cuxton
Mrs E. A. Wharton
Keith White, Chatham
Ruby A. White, Chatham
P. R. Wilder
Ann & Norman Williams, Chatham
Brian Williams, Chatham
Veronica Williams, Wigmore
Willaim J. Willis, Gillingham
Robert J. Hendry Winter, Chatham
Fay Woodhams

FRITH PRODUCTS & SERVICES

Francis Frith would doubtless be pleased to know that the pioneering publishing venture he started in 1860 still continues today. Over a hundred and forty years later, The Francis Frith Collection continues in the same innovative tradition and is now one of the foremost publishers of vintage photographs in the world. Some of the current activities include:

INTERIOR DECORATION

Today Frith's photographs can be seen framed and as giant wall murals in thousands of pubs, restaurants, hotels, banks, retail stores and other public buildings throughout the country. In every case they enhance the unique local atmosphere of the places they depict and provide reminders of gentler days in an increasingly busy and frenetic world.

PRODUCT PROMOTIONS

Frith products are used by many major companies to promote the sales of their own products or to reinforce their own history and heritage. Frith promotions have been used by Hovis bread, Courage beers, Scots Porage Oats, Colman's mustard, Cadbury's foods, Mellow Birds coffee, Dunhill pipe tobacco, Guinness, and Bulmer's Cider.

GENEALOGY AND FAMILY HISTORY

As the interest in family history and roots grows world-wide, more and more people are turning to Frith's photographs of Great Britain for images of the towns, villages and streets where their ancestors lived; and, of course, photographs of the churches and chapels where their ancestors were christened, married and buried are an essential part of every genealogy tree and family album.

FRITH PRODUCTS

All Frith photographs are available Framed or just as Mounted Prints and unmounted versions. These may be ordered from the address below. Other products available are - Calendars, Jigsaws, Canvas Prints, Mugs, Tea Towels, Tableware and local and prestige books.

THE INTERNET

Over several hundred thousand Frith photographs can be viewed and purchased on the internet through the Frith websites!

For more detailed information on Frith products, look at
www.francisfrith.com

See the complete list of Frith Books at: www.francisfrith.com
This web site is regularly updated with the latest list of publications from The Francis Frith Collection. If you wish to buy books relating to another part of the country that your local bookshop does not stock, you may purchase on-line.

For further information, trade, or author enquiries please contact us at the address below:
The Francis Frith Collection, Unit 19 Kingsmead Business Park, Gillingham, Dorset SP8 5FB.
Tel: +44 (0)1722 716 376   Email: sales@francisfrith.co.uk

See Frith products on the internet at www.francisfrith.com

FREE PRINT OF YOUR CHOICE
CHOOSE A PHOTOGRAPH FROM THIS BOOK
+ POSTAGE

Mounted Print
Overall size 14 x 11 inches (355 x 280mm)

TO RECEIVE YOUR FREE PRINT

Choose any Frith photograph in this book

Simply complete the Voucher opposite and return it with your payment (to cover postage and handling) and we will print the photograph of your choice in SEPIA (size 11 x 8 inches) and supply it in a cream mount ready to frame (overall size 14 x 11 inches).

Order additional Mounted Prints at HALF PRICE - £19.00 each (normally £38.00)

If you would like to order more Frith prints from this book, possibly as gifts for friends and family, you can buy them at half price (with no additional postage costs).

Have your Mounted Prints framed

For an extra £20.00 per print you can have your mounted print(s) framed in an elegant polished wood and gilt moulding, overall size 16 x 13 inches (no additional postage required).

IMPORTANT!

❶ Please note: aerial photographs and photographs with a reference number starting with a "Z" are not Frith photographs and cannot be supplied under this offer.

❷ Offer valid for delivery to one UK address only.

❸ These special prices are only available if you use this form to order. You must use the ORIGINAL VOUCHER on this page (no copies permitted). We can only despatch to one UK address.

❹ This offer cannot be combined with any other offer.

As a customer your name & address will be stored by Frith but not sold or rented to third parties. Your data will be used for the purpose of this promotion only.

Send completed Voucher form to:
**The Francis Frith Collection,
1 Chilmark Estate House, Chilmark,
Salisbury, Wiltshire SP3 5DU**

Voucher *for FREE and Reduced Price Frith Prints*

Please do not photocopy this voucher. Only the original is valid, so please fill it in, cut it out and return it to us with your order.

Picture ref no	Page no	Qty	Mounted @ £19.00	Framed + £20.00	Total Cost £
		1	Free of charge*	£	£
			£19.00	£	£
			£19.00	£	£
			£19.00	£	£
			£19.00	£	£
			£19.00	£	£
Please allow 28 days for delivery. Offer available to one UK address only.			* Post & handling		£3.80
			Total Order Cost		£

Title of this book ....

I enclose a cheque/postal order for £ ....
made payable to 'Heritage Resource Management Ltd'

OR please debit my Mastercard / Visa / Maestro card, details below

Card Number:

Issue No (Maestro only):   Valid from (Maestro):

Card Security Number: Expires:

Signature:

Name Mr/Mrs/Ms ....

Address ....

....

....

.... Postcode ....

Daytime Tel No ....

Email ....

Valid to 31/12/26

Free Print – see overleaf

Can you help us with information about any of the Frith photographs in this book?

We are gradually compiling an historical record for each of the photographs in the Frith archive. It is always fascinating to find out the names of the people shown in the pictures, as well as insights into the shops, buildings and other features depicted.

If you recognize anyone in the photographs in this book, or if you have information not already included in the author's caption, do let us know. We would love to hear from you, and will try to publish it in future books or articles.

An Invitation from The Francis Frith Collection to Share Your Memories

The 'Share Your Memories' feature of our website allows members of the public to add personal memories relating to the places featured in our photographs, or comment on others already added. Seeing a place from your past can rekindle forgotten or long held memories. Why not visit the website, find photographs of places you know well and add YOUR story for others to read and enjoy? We would love to hear from you!

www.francisfrith.com/memories

Our production team

Frith books are produced by a small dedicated team at offices near Salisbury. Most have worked with the Frith Collection for many years. All have in common one quality: they have a passion for the Frith Collection.

Frith Books and Gifts

We have a wide range of books and gifts available on our website utilising our photographic archive, many of which can be individually personalised.

www.francisfrith.com